THE SAAMI OF LAPLAND

Piers Vitebsky

Thomson Learning
New York

Books in the series

Kalahari Bushmen
Kurds
Maori
Native Americans
Saami of Lapland
Tibetans

Published by Steck-Vaughn
Australian Aborigines
Bedouin
Inuit
Rainforest Amerindians

For Catherine

Series editor: Paul Mason
Designer: Kudos Editorial and Design Services

Picture acknowledgments
The artwork on pages 6 and 38 was supplied by Peter Bull. The publishers gratefully acknowledge the permission of the following to use their pictures: Bryan and Cherry Alexander 5, 8, 15 (bottom), 18, 19, 20, 22, 23, 24, 25, 26 (both), 28, 32, 35, 44, 45; Britstock 13, 16; Camera Press 21, 29, 44; Eye Ubiquitous 10 (both), 29, 31, 37, 41, 42; Robert Harding 4,11; Hutchison Library 30, 39; Impact 14; Magnum 7, 34, 43; Mansell Collection 12; John Massey-Stewart 27, 33; Rex Features 40 (bottom); Tony Stone Worldwide cover, 9, 15 (top), 36; Topham 17, 40 (top).

First published in the United States by
Thomson Learning
115 Fifth Avenue
New York, NY 10003

First published in 1993 by
Wayland (Publishers) Ltd

Library of Congress Cataloging-in-Publication Data applied for

ISBN 1-56847-159-9

Printed in Italy

Contents

Who are the Saami? 4

Landscape and ecology 9

The Saami at home 18

Culture and religion 26

Ethnic identity today 35

Glossary 46

Further information 47

Further reading 47

Index 48

1 Who are the Saami?

. . . Two men in bright blue costume with red trim stand in the middle of a corral, surrounded by a swirling herd of reindeer. Each one holds a lasso coiled in his hand and occasionally casts it out over the antlers of a deer he wants to catch in order to separate it from the others . . . On a dark winter's day, a heavily wrapped herder drives a huge herd of reindeer from one hilltop to another, steering his snowmobile from side to side behind them, rounding up stragglers . . . Inside a crowded tent, a woman, also in red and blue, and with a shawl over her shoulders, serves mugs of hot coffee to the herders as they enter, tired and hungry.

Anyone who knows Norway, Sweden, or Finland can picture these scenes in their minds; they are also shown often in tourist brochures and posters. But who are the Saami (pronounced Sar-mee), or Lapp, people? The herding of reindeer is only one of the occupations of these

▲ *A herder stands in the swirling snow and mist, surrounded by reindeer. Reindeer live in cold climates so their herders must work outside in all kinds of weather. This man is holding a lasso, an essential tool for catching reindeer.*

▲ *A family in northern Norway relaxing inside their tent. Traditionally the whole family traveled together with the herds, but today this is difficult because the children have to attend school. The man has just come in and still has his lasso wound around his shoulder.*

people from the far north of Europe, and not even the commonest. Other Saami live by fishing in the mountain rivers and lakes, or in the Norwegian fjords and on the open sea beyond. Still others work in factories, drive trucks, teach in schools, or do one of a hundred other jobs.

The Saami are a people spread over four countries: Norway, Sweden, Finland, and the part of Russia bordering Scandinavia. It is not easy to know how many of them there are, since for a long time neighboring peoples made them feel ashamed of being Saami; many of them concealed their true origins and changed their way of life to that of their neighbors.

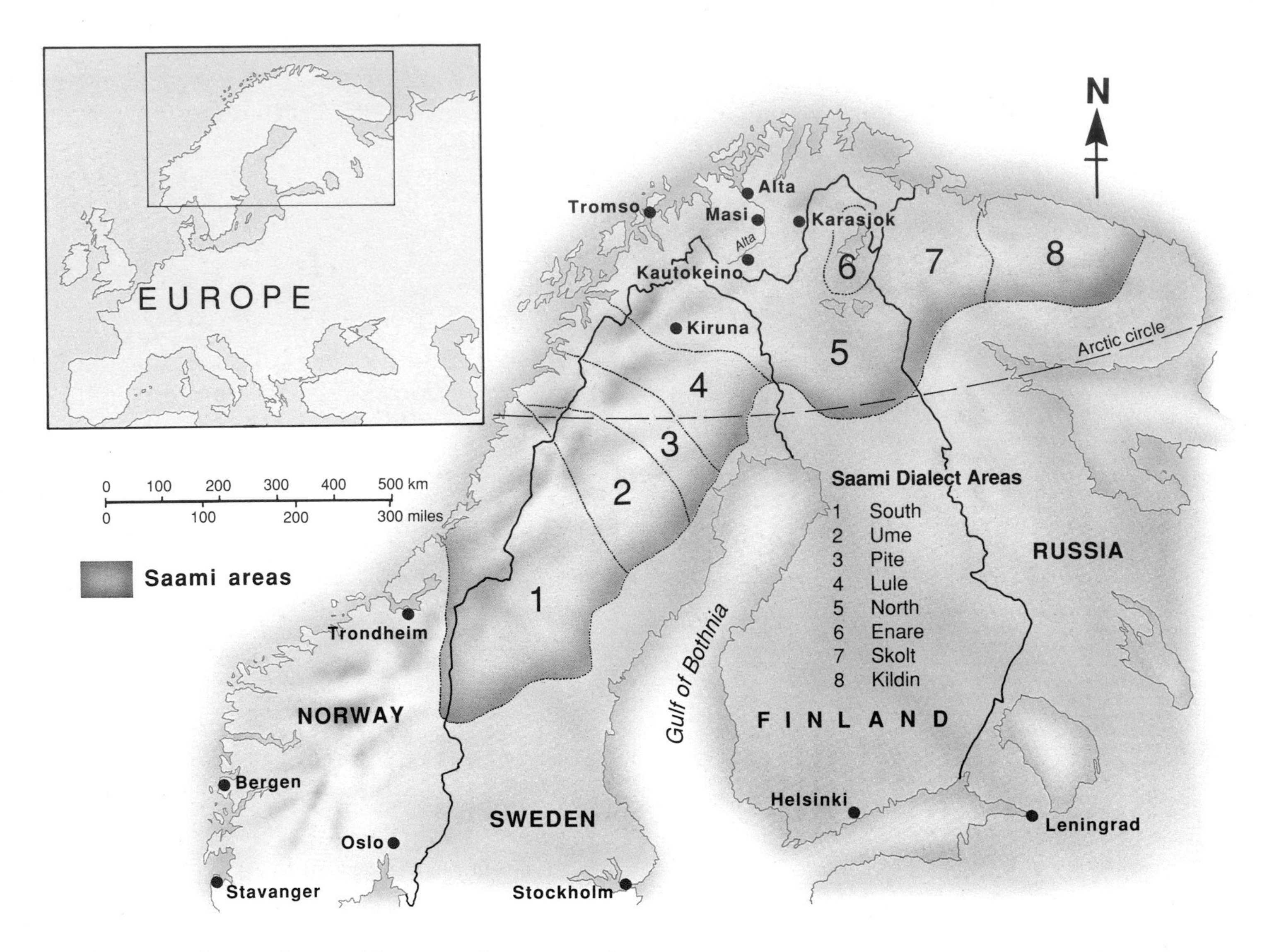

The Saami are often said to number around 35,000, with 20,000 of these in Norway, 10,000 in Sweden, 3,000-4,000 in Finland and 1,000-2,000 in Russia. But other estimates put the total number of Saami at up to 300,000. Certainly, the figure of 35,000 is likely to increase as people become more proud of being Saami and willing to admit their background.

The name Lapp has been used by neighboring peoples to describe the Saami, but the Saami do not like it: they consider it insulting. Their name for Lapland is *Sapme* or *Same Ätnam*. Where the Saami came from is uncertain, but theories range from northern Russia to central Asia. Their language is related to Finnish, Hungarian, and Estonian. However, there are considerable differences among the Saami in various regions.

An ancient people

Over a thousand years ago Alfred the Great, the King of England, wrote that the Norwegian chief Ottar sailed northward on and on up the Norwegian coast. "*He said that he wished to find out how far the land extended northwards, or whether anyone lived to the north of the wilderness.*" At the farthest point he turned back at a place where the people seemed unfriendly because "*he dared not sail on past the river for fear of hostility.*" On the way he saw how the Saami used tame reindeer as decoys to capture wild reindeer by luring them toward humans. Some Saami paid the Norwegian chiefs taxes. They paid in "*skins, bird's feathers, and ship's ropes made from the hide of whales and seals.*"

The Saami were mentioned around 100 A.D. by the Roman author Tacitus, who also wrote about the tribes of ancient Germany and Britain. Around 870 A.D., Alfred the Great of England received a visit from a Norwegian chieftain named Ottar who lived in the far north of what is now Norway. Ottar told Alfred that the Saami kept reindeer herds, though these were probably much smaller than today's. It is certain that the Saami occupied northern Scandinavia long before the Finns, Swedes, or Norwegians, who lived in the south of these countries and moved north only later. This fact is important for the Saami when they claim today that they, and not the governments in the south, should control what happens in their homeland. Saami insist that they are aboriginal, which means the people who were there first.

Though some districts and parishes in the Saami area are populated almost entirely by Saami, they form only a tiny minority of the populations of Scandinavian countries. Even in

A Saami man grilling freshwater fish on the bank of a river. Like many Saami he wears modern factory clothes, although in really cold weather these are not as warm as traditional furs. ▶

▲ *The church at Kautokeino, in the heart of Norwegian Saami territory, during winter. At this season it remains dark all day, but the snow reflects a great deal of light. At the front of the picture is a household's supply of firewood and equipment, covered with snow.*

the north, there are large industrial towns inhabited by outsiders: the total population of the region is well over two million. Also, many Saami have moved away from the north to work in Oslo or other southern cities.

Many Saami, in fact the large majority, live in a way that seems almost exactly the same as their Scandinavian neighbors. Some look different, while many look like other Scandinavians. For the most part, they even wear the same clothes, live in the same kind of houses, and do the same jobs: fishing, farming, or factory work. Yet whether they are proud of it or ashamed of it, Saami are keenly aware of their Saami origin. The situation is similar in some ways to that of the Welsh in Britain, the Bretons in France, or the Basques in France and Spain.

Because they are divided among four countries, it has been hard for the Saami to maintain constant contact and set up common organizations. Until the reforms begun by the Russian leader Gorbachev in the late 1980s, there was almost no contact between the Saami in Russia and those outside. However, the Saami of the other three countries have joined together in the Nordic Saami Council. In 1973 this council founded the Nordic Saami Institute in the village of Kautokeino in Norway. This institute promotes the study of Saami language and culture and is set in the heart of reindeer-herding country. Norway is also the country where Saami culture may be said to be strongest, and because of this most of the examples in this book will be taken from there.

2 Landscape and ecology

Much of Saami territory lies north of the Arctic Circle, with dark, cold winters and light, warm summers. The country is mostly forested up to a point in the north beyond which trees will not grow. This point is called the tree line; the land beyond the tree line as far as the sea is called tundra. The tundra is covered with low-growing plants such as grasses, mosses and lichens, berries and dwarf shrubs. Taller plants and trees could not withstand the icy winds that come in off the sea. Farther south, where the land is forested, winters are still long and harsh, and the plants have only a short summer period when they can grow. So the people who use this land must do so carefully.

The midnight sun

The Arctic Circle is an imaginary line drawn on the map at 66°33' north. On midsummer night the land near the Arctic Circle, because the north pole is tilted toward the sun, does not rotate away from the sun. The sun does not set below the horizon, but shines all through the night. As you get closer to the north pole, the summer nights get lighter and lighter and the sun does not set for several days or even weeks. On the other hand, there is one day in midwinter when the land near the Arctic Circle does not face the sun at all. Farther north, the sun is well below the horizon, so there is no sunshine for days or weeks; it never gets very light in winter.

◀ *The tundra in autumn. Snow already covers the mountains, and on the tundra the dwarf willows and other shrubs prepare to lose their leaves. The low-growing yellow-green plant on the ground is lichen.*

◀ ▲ *Preparing reindeer carcasses. The herders slaughter a few to eat throughout the year, but most of the meat is sold to traders from the towns. The inner organs are also eaten: there are many traditonal Saami recipes for them.*

If reindeer are allowed to graze for too long on the same pasture, it will take years for the plants to grow back again. Lichen, on which the deer depend in the winter, takes thirty years to grow back. So reindeer herds must be kept constantly on the move.

Hunting, fishing, farming, and herding make tough demands, and people need an intimate knowledge of how animals, the weather, and the landscape behave. The early inhabitants lived entirely by hunting and fishing. Many people who still live on the land now grow some crops, especially on the coast. Food from elsewhere is also available in stores and supermarkets, although it is expensive. In earlier times, no one could get enough food in the Arctic except by eating animals and fish. This diet also gives the high proportion of protein and energy needed in the cold climate. Animal skins, bones, and horns traditionally provided the main materials for making clothing, tools, and other equipment, and they remain important today.

The pattern of traditional Saami life revolves around the seasons. Whereas most town-dwellers think of only four seasons – spring, summer, autumn, and winter – the reindeer-herding Saami divide the year into eight seasons, based on their own experiences of the landscape. What they call "early spring" is the time when it starts to get light but the snow is still several feet deep. The next season, "spring," is when dazzling sunshine spreads over the snowy ground and the reindeer calves are born. In "early summer," which is not until late May or early June, the last of the winter's snow finally melts and the rivers are filled with rushing water. "Summer" is the season around midsummer. Now it stays light constantly and children can play out of doors all night. But in summer there are also hordes of midges and mosquitos. It is already "late summer" when the bilberries ripen, as well as the cloudberries, which are a sort of yellow raspberry. By now, it is already getting cooler and chilly mists are beginning to close in. In "autumn," much of the landscape turns to brown and gold, as grass starts to die and the leaves change color on all the smaller trees and shrubs. This is the time of the main slaughter of the herd. Some of the animals fattened up on the summer pastures are sold for meat; others are kept to face the tough winter ahead. In "late autumn," everyone moves toward the "winter" pasture, where the deep snow deadens sound and the entire landscape is calm and silent. Even at midday it hardly gets light at all, and in the far north, above the Arctic Circle, it remains dark all day and all night for several weeks. However, the snow on the ground reflects some light and one can read a newspaper outside for two or three hours at midday.

To move around on this landscape of bog, forest, and snow requires special forms of

Because the seasons change rapidly and the weather is extreme, the herder Saami divide the year into many more seasons than town dwellers. This picture shows a mountain stream in the season known as early summer. The force of the rushing mountain streams has encouraged governments to build hydroelectric dams. These dams ruin the reindeer herders' pastures and have led to widespread protests from Saami and environmentalists. ▶

transportation. The Saami are said to have invented skis; archaeologists have found Saami skis that are 3,500 years old. Saami nowadays use mass-produced skis from stores, but traditional Saami skis were made of wood, often with a strip of reindeer fur on the underside with the hairs pointing backward. The hairs allowed greater speed going downhill, while acting as a brake against slipping backward when going uphill. Reindeer herders also use sleds pulled by reindeer. These sleds carry both luggage and passengers. Saami do not ride on the backs of reindeer, the way other reindeer-herding peoples do farther east in Russia. Snowmobiles are essential for herders and people also use them in winter to get around in town, much as they might use motorcycles elsewhere. There are also all-terrain vehicles with tracks like a tank's, though these damage the land. Many families also have cars, and there are well surfaced roads throughout most of the region along which buses travel.

The Saami occupy several distinct kinds of environment: mountain, forest, lake, and coast. Each supports a different group of Saami with a distinctive economy and culture.

REINDEER-HERDING SAAMI

The best-known Saami are the reindeer herders described at the beginning of this book. Reindeer herders are largely nomadic. This means that they do not live in one place, but migrate at various seasons of the year from one pasture to another. Reindeer are sensitive animals, so the herders migrate in order to provide their deer with the right weather and the right kind of plants to graze on at each season. Their migrations form an annual cycle, so they come back to the

▲ *A picture from an early travel book. The public in southern cities was fascinated by exotic reports of the peoples of the far north, and they loved to hear tales of fur-clad Saami moving about the frozen landscape on their skis or in "ice boats," as sleds were called.*

◀ *A Chukchi reindeer herder from the far northeast of Siberia, near the Bering Strait. About two and a half million of the world's three million domestic reindeer are in northern Russia, where they are herded by many of the region's thirty different aboriginal peoples.*

same place at the same time each year.

Some reindeer-herding Saami are called forest Saami. They live in the lower-lying forests of Sweden, where they make short seasonal migrations with their relatively small herds. These Saami fish and grow crops, as well as herd reindeer. But the most spectacular form of reindeer herding is done by the mountain Saami who are based in the interior mountains of Sweden and Norway. These people travel up to 250 miles each spring from their inland base to their summer pastures on the Atlantic coast. In autumn they travel back again to their winter pastures. In Finland there are many non-Saami reindeer herders and in Russia about twenty other peoples apart from the Saami herd reindeer. But in Sweden and Norway reindeer herding has a unique significance for Saami identity: by law, in these countries the Saami alone are allowed to herd reindeer. Though only about 10 per cent of Saami live by reindeer herding, it has thus become a symbol of the Saami people as a whole.

Reindeer originally lived in Arctic North America and crossed into Asia and Europe in prehistoric times, when Siberia was still joined to Alaska across what is now the Bering Strait. The Arctic peoples of Asia and the Saami in Europe domesticated the reindeer; today in these regions there are 3 million domesticated reindeer, far more than the number of wild ones. But they were never domesticated in North America, where there are still enormous herds of wild reindeer called caribou.

COASTAL SAAMI

The belief among outsiders that only reindeer herders are true Saami causes problems. Apart from the lake Saami, who live by fishing in lakes and rivers, the other main group of Saami is the coastal Saami. The coastal communities are far larger than the communities of reindeer herders. They live along the Norwegian coast, where most of them have been settled for centuries. The coastal Saami do not herd reindeer; they make their living partly by sea fishing and farming, but increasingly in factories and in jobs such as driving buses and trucks. They are thus employed in nontraditional occupations, in typical jobs of industrial society. The coastal Saami therefore have a way of life that is hardly different from the lives of the more numerous Norwegians in the same areas.

The history of the coastal Saami has been very different from the history of the reindeer-herding Saami, though there has always been close contact between them. They live on a

◀ *Oks fjord in the far north of Norway. Both Saami and Norwegian fishermen live here. The members of the crew of a fishing boat each take a share of the catch, with the boat's owner taking the largest share. Fishermen may work in different boats with various partners from year to year, but Saami boats often belong to a traditional work group called the si'ida.*

▲ *Houses beside a lake. The whole of Lapland is criss-crossed with lakes.*

stormy coast with deep inlets called fjords (pronounced fee-ord') which wind inland for anything up to 60 miles. These fjords reach in between steep, high mountains that often plunge straight into the water. Out to sea, beyond the fjords, there are numerous islands. Villages and farms are sheltered by the winding fjords from the wild storms outside. Though the coastal Saami used to hunt wild reindeer on land, much of their work has always been sea fishing.

Because communications run along the coast, the coastal Saami had close contact with Norwegians from the south; with Russian traders who sailed down around the top of Norway; and with sailors from England, Scotland, Holland, and other countries. Norwegian settlers have been moving farther north for hundreds of years,

▲ *A man prepared to go ice fishing. The drill is used to make a hole in the ice, the barrel is for storing fish.*

◀ *Cod hanging out to dry on the Norwegian coast. Drying is an ancient form of preservation that was invented long before people had refrigerators. The coastal Saami also catch halibut, salmon, coalfish, and capelin: the fishermen know that coalfish and capelin have arrived when they see the gulls swooping down to pick them out of the water.*

and before the nineteenth century they already outnumbered the coastal Saami. These settlers lived – like the coastal Saami – by fishing and farming.

During the course of this century, the coastal Saami have begun to fish less and farm more. A generation or two ago, the focus of a village was the water's edge, where the nets and the fish were strung out to dry and the boats were drawn up ready to set out at a moment's notice. The Saami fishermen would sit at the window carefully watching the surface of the water for the first sign of fish movement in the fjord.

Fishing is still important today, but most households also spend much of their time farming. A typical life-style now is for a man to spend the winter and spring out at sea on a fishing boat and the summer months tending his sheep and cattle on the narrow meadows around the fjord. One of the most important tasks is to lay in enough hay for the women to feed the animals in winter, since the animals cannot graze on lichen throughout the winter like reindeer. There is often not enough work, and it is very expensive to run your own boat. So young, unmarried men in particular travel up and down the coast to find work on other people's boats. They also work in factories and in the tourist industry, since the entire Saami area attracts a large number of tourists from the south and from abroad.

Farming along the fjords is precarious, and there is a risk that when the mountain Saami arrive in the summer with their reindeer, the deer may trample and eat the grasses that the coastal Saami need for their cattle and sheep. This can create hostility between coastal and mountain Saami. Many coastal Saami are also unhappy that when the rest of the world thinks of the Saami, it thinks first of the reindeer herders. The two groups of Saami try to stay on good terms with each other, but the growing gulf between their life-styles is reflected in a split between different Saami political parties.

The Saami and their land are vulnerable to a number of threats. Tourism brings money into the area, but "tourists just regard us as a curiosity," as one woman put it. "They don't treat us with proper respect. Weekend hunters and fishermen come from the town just for sport and kill the game birds and fish we need for our food. On lonely roads where no one's looking, they're so cheeky [bold] they'll even shoot a reindeer and drive off with it in the boot [trunk] of their car." Though it is against the law in Norway, even the berries on which the local people rely for their fruit supply are picked by outsiders. But the main threats come from industrial developments such as mining projects and hydroelectric dams. These raise great political storms and will be discussed in chapter 5.

Saami distinguish between different kinds of snow, and older Saami even say that these have different effects on the body. For example, frostbite occurs when part of your flesh becomes frozen through exposure to the cold. It can just leave a mark on your skin like a burn or it can lead to the loss of a whole limb. *The moment you see that any part is frozen,* wrote the old hunter and herder Johan Turi, *you must rub and knead it with snow until the blood comes back and life comes into it. But the topmost snow does not help at all, but it must be the snow called saenjas* (a more grainy kind of snow), *and that kind of snow always lies nearest the ground.*

▲ *Tourists on the deck of a Norwegian cruise ship. Tourism brings money to Saami regions but can also cause problems, since weekend hunters kill the animals and fish some Saami need for food.*

3 The Saami at home

▲ *A Saami family at home in Sweden. Although people often think that Saami live out on the land in tents with the reindeer herds, more Saami actually live in houses just like those of other Scandinavians.*

Saami life is a mixture of some features familiar from the rest of northern Europe and others that are quite distinctive. Unless they are reindeer herders on migration, most Saami live in modern, comfortable houses. They have television sets, cars, and large freezers full of meat (though the standard of living is much lower in Russia). A teenager's bedroom may have posters of international rock stars on the wall, as well as a trophy made from reindeer antlers. Garden sheds are full of fur clothes for the winter, logs for the stove, and spare parts for the snowmobile. In a coastal Saami village, the yard may be littered with boats, motors, and nets. In the herding areas, there may be piles of reindeer antlers outside the door, and a modern bathroom may have the legs of slaughtered reindeer stacked up against the shower unit.

The towns and villages contain stores, bus stops, cafes, and bars. In winter, you can see teenagers roaring up and down the streets and across the nearby hillsides on snowmobiles. On a winter evening, when everyone is indoors, the streets of even the liveliest village can seem deathly quiet until you open a door and enter a crowded nightclub.

Reindeer herders on the move in summer still use the traditional tent (*lavvo*), and in many areas you can still see a few of the old type of wooden or turf winter houses. But there are not many old houses, especially in northern Norway. During World War II, the German army burned down much of this area as it retreated. When the war was over, the government embarked on a massive rebuilding program. The new houses were built in the same sort of style as houses in the rest of the country. At the same time the government built much of the road network, which is better than in any other area of the Arctic. These developments sped up the changes in the Saami way of life and brought even the remotest areas within easier reach of stores and money.

Though many kinds of southern foods are available in stores and supermarkets, they come from far away and are expensive. People still make great use of local meat and fish because they are cheaper. In the cities of the south, reindeer meat is considered unusual and exotic, but for many Saami in the north it is their staple diet. The main slaughter of reindeer is in the autumn and winter, but the herders slaughter an

▲ *A tame reindeer visits the village shop. Small local stores sell newspapers, food, hardware, and other useful things such as batteries. This customer prefers chocolate.*

animal from time to time as they need it. Meat is preserved by salting it and hanging it up to dry, though freezers are also used. A sausage called *marfi* made from blood and fat is also popular. Saami drink a lot of very strong coffee.

The traditional work group is called a *si'ida*. The *si'ida* (pronounced see-eeda) includes a number of families, with mother, father, and children, and maybe also uncles, aunts, and other relatives. These people live and work together in herding or fishing. Among reindeer herders, families in the *si'ida* own their own reindeer but manage a joint herd. The deer are easier to manage like this and are also better protected against wild animals. Among coastal fishermen, the *si'ida* is made up of men who work a fishing boat. This kind of working organization evolved in a hunting and fishing economy in a vast, wild region, where cooperation was necessary between scattered people. There were also local councils made up of one man from each family. Now that so many

▲ *A herder warms his hands at the fire. The* lavvo *is made with a circular framework of poles leaning inward, like that of a teepee or wigwam. The floor is usually made of birch twigs covered with several layers of reindeer fur, and the fire is laid on flat stones.*

▲ *The view from a sled as a Saami herder travels over the snowy lands toward the summer pasture. The sun, in the early spring, has appeared above the horizon.*

Saami have stopped herding or fishing the *si'ida* has become weaker, but it still survives among reindeer herding families.

Though coastal and mountain Saami live mostly separate lives, they keep in touch and exchange information and help. Traditionally, each *si'ida* of herders in Finnmark formed a relationship with a family of coastal Saami. They set out for the summer pasture knowing that their friends were expecting them at their destination. These relationships are now fading.

In late winter, while it is still very cold and dark, the herders keep a watch on the weather and listen to the radio forecasts. When they judge that the right time has come, they pack up the poles and canvas of their *lavvo* and load everything on sleds. The reindeer that pull the sleds are mostly strong castrated males, which can be trained easily.

The male and female deer may be separated and made to travel in two groups. After their winter diet of lichen, the males are eager to go in search of fresh pasture and move naturally and quickly in the direction called *davveli*, which means away from the winter pasture and toward the summer grazing grounds. "But often, we hold them back to give a start to the herd of females," explains a young herder. "They need special care. The females become restless if we herd them alongside the males and are more relaxed if we just keep them with other females." The calves will be born in the spring; the pregnant females must be prevented from scattering and helped to find a sheltered spot to give birth to their calves. Here they use their hooves to scrape a hollow in the snow for the calves to be born in. The calves are generally born in early May. The mothers try to protect their offspring from predators and scavengers such as eagles, ravens, foxes, and wolves.

Several *si'idas*, each including their own herds, may follow the same route to the coast. The herders of each *si'ida* try to occupy the same calving ground each year, but they may have to compete with others; the first group to arrive at a particular site has the right to stay there.

While on the move, the herders often travel by night and stop in the morning to eat and sleep. The daytime sun melts the surface of the snow, making it too soft for the heavily laden sleds. But at night the surface of the snow freezes up again.

It is bitterly cold and the herders drink plenty of strong black coffee. The male herd takes the main baggage on a caravan of sleds, while the

▲ *Saami in Norway using snowmobiles to herd reindeer. A snowmobile has a runner like a ski at the front and two caterpillar tracks behind. It can run along a frozen main road as well as climb steep, rough ground. Supplies and equipment are pulled behind on sleds.*

▲ *Driving reindeer into a corral. The tamest reindeer are the leaders; they wear bells and are followed by the rest of the herd. Sometimes a leader may be taken into the corral and the remainder of the herd will follow, but usually they are driven from behind. Here, they are running away from the fluttering sackcloth, which drives them forward.*

herd of pregnant females travels light. Pack deer carry the herders' *lavvo*. In the past, the women and children of the *si'ida* traveled along with the men and the deer, but now they usually go on ahead by bus or car all the way to the area of the summer camp to prepare the site. This journey usually takes them only one or two days.

As soon as possible after the calves are born, the herds move on toward the summer pastures. From around mid-May, depending on how far north they are, the sun never dips below the horizon and it stays light all night. There may still be occasional snowstorms, but the grass and other vegetation are now growing and the snow is melting fast. The herders must decide whether to wait for the newborn calves to get stronger or to move on before the rivers on the way are made dangerous or impassable by floods of meltwater from the mountains.

At last, around midsummer, they reach the summer pastures. These lie on the coastal hills or even on one of the many offshore islands. In the past, the herds of deer were driven into the water and made to swim across: now, the Norwegian navy ferries the animals across.

The few herders who watched over the calving are joined by other members of their families who have been driving the male herd behind them, and who have kept in close contact. Their *lavvo*, quick and easy to put up and take down again, is replaced by a bigger, more comfortable family tent.

The herders have now reached the land of their coastal Saami hosts who, if all goes well, meet them with a warm welcome. Over many a long summer evening's eating and drinking, they swap stories. The herders recount their adventures on their trek across the mountains, while their hosts talk about their adventures on the open sea during the winter and spring fishing season, or discuss politics, the prospects for employment, and the activities of mutual friends and acquaintances. The herding women have already been in the area for some time and have worked hard at arranging the camp and renewing friendships. Because of this they are often better at speaking Norwegian than the men.

Toys and games

Children often play by imitating the activities of adults. Nowadays, Saami children mostly have the same toys as children anywhere else in Europe. But they also use some things that are not found elsewhere. In reindeer herding camps, children pretend that pairs of antlers are real reindeer and carry them around, herding the "reindeer" from one place to another. Sometimes children hold the antlers on top of their heads and run around pretending to be reindeer, while others try to capture them with lassos. They also play a version of blind man's bluff, where the blindfolded person is a monster called Stallo who tries to catch and eat the others.

▲ *Deer swimming toward the summer pastures on the Norwegian coast. They usually follow a leader deer into the water. Although the male deer may have arrived earlier, it takes the females and young calves two or three weeks to reach here from the calving grounds. The deer risk drowning, so today the Norwegian navy often ferries the deer across.*

▲ *At the end of the spring migration, a herd of reindeer arrives at the summer pastures. Here, the herders must take care to respect the farmland of the coastal Saami inhabitants in order to avoid quarrels that occur when reindeer break down fences or eat crops.*

Some of the coast-dwellers may be inland Saami who have given up reindeer herding because of the shortage of pasture and employment in the mountains. Sometimes, there are marriages between members of the two groups. Herders also often ask their hosts to act as godparents to their children. This ensures that the friendly relations between their families will continue into the next generation.

The Saami on the coast speak mostly Norwegian, so the herders speak Norwegian with them. The herding children play both with children from their own *si'ida* and with the Norwegian-speaking children of their host families. The children gossip and joke with each other. These playful relations also help to prevent quarrels. If reindeer get out of control and trample the hosts' fields or break down the surrounding fences, it is usually the women, with their better command of Norwegian, who go to apologize and smooth it over. They take the children to make the visit more informal.

4 Culture and religion

The traditional Saami way of life is based on nature: they make their living from the land on which they live. Traditionally things such as the Saami's clothing and handicrafts, their religion or ideas about the place of human beings in the world, and their language are directly influenced by their natural surroundings.

▲ *Two styles of Saami costume in Sweden (above) and Norway (above right). Every Saami region has its own distinctive style and patterns.*

CLOTHING AND HANDICRAFTS

Traditional clothes are sewn by women. In the mountains, these are the famous blue and red designs in summer and coats and leggings made of fur in winter. "You can tell exactly where anyone comes from if you know the costume," explains a woman in Karasjok, Norway. "Our men have a three-pointed hat, while down in Rørøs the hat goes straight up and round at the top. Over in Sweden, in Karasuando, the hat is covered with a huge bobble." The clothing you wear is the clearest way of showing other people who you are. Until a few years ago, it was widely said by Norwegians, Swedes, Finns, and Russians that the Saami were primitive and backward, and Saami were often made to feel ashamed of their identity. Many Saami therefore abandoned their costume and started wearing the ordinary clothes of their neighbors in order to look the same. Recently, however, a new generation of Saami has taken to wearing the traditional costumes in public as well as at home. So there is a strange situation: a Saami wearing traditional costume may be either an old-fashioned person who never gave it up, or a new-style supporter of Saami cultural freedom. Particularly among writers, artists, and intellectuals, but also among many other people, it has become fashionable to wear Saami costume on important occasions and even every day.

In the old days, Saami used to tell stories about the origins of the sun, the moon, and the stars. The Saami in Russia used to tell this story. *There once lived a girl who could run very fast. In another village there lived a boy who could also run fast. He heard about the girl and made up his mind to marry her. The girl ran away into the forest and the boy followed her. She kept on running ahead of him and he could not catch up with her, so he thought of a cunning plan. He chased her up a mountain until she reached the top and had nowhere farther to go. So she jumped up into the air. He could not see her anywhere and collapsed to the ground exhausted and in despair. The girl came down again to earth and took pity on him. To revive him, she poured some milk between the boy's lips. But the wind took the milk and spread it across the sky, where it turned into silver and became the milky way. The wind turned the girl to silver as well. So the boy could not marry her and returned to his village broken-hearted.*

▲ *A wall decoration by schoolchildren in Sevettijarvi, Finland, with figures in Saami costume. Throughout Lapland, schools have often left Saami culture out of children's lessons, so they have become cut off from their roots, but this has recently changed in some places.*

◀ *A craftsman fits a knife handle made from reindeer antler to the blade. Both the handles and the sheaths can be made out of wood or antler. The handle may be inlaid with patterns in birch bark or leather.*

Before the spread of industrial society and manufactured goods from the south, the Saami had to make everything they needed from the animals, stones, and trees that were available locally. In particular, Saami have always made their own tools. They have made skis for thousands of years. Before they began to use larger seagoing power boats at the beginning of this century, coastal Saami fishermen made their own boats. Herders make tents from poles and canvas (earlier, they used reindeer skins), houses from logs and turf, knife-handles from antlers, and clothes and shoes from reindeer fur, sewn with tough thread made from reindeer sinews. The iron blades of knives used to be made by blacksmiths, who were regarded as having great magical power because of their mysterious craft.

These articles are often beautifully decorated. Saami craftsmen do this for themselves or for other Saami, and there is no dividing line between what they make for practical purposes and what they make for artistic reasons. But Saami handicrafts are also popular among tourists and their sale contributes a great deal to the local economy. The finest work is often kept for their own use instead of being sold.

RELIGION

A people's culture does not exist only in things you can hold in your hand. Culture is also something that exists in one's mind. It is part of how a person understands the world.

In earliest times, Saami believed in a number of spirits of the sun, the moon, and various parts of the landscape around them. The seasons, the

The *joik* (pronounced yoik) is a special Saami form of singing. It is made up on the spot without instruments and can be sung anywhere out in the wilds. You make up a joik about an animal, a person or even the land and the weather by singing a few affectionate or teasing words about them, or about something they have done, mixed with nonsense words. For a long time, people have been giving up joiking because it was considered old-fashioned. Now pop groups are working joiks into their songs and they are becoming very popular again.

health and fertility of humans and animals, the kindness or harshness of the elements – all of these were believed to come from the world of spirits. A male spirit-medium called in English a shaman, or in Saami *noiade*, helped people to avoid misfortune. This was a talent that only a few people had. By beating a special drum in a dramatic performance, the *noiade* could go into a state of trance in order to communicate with the world of the spirits and find out which spirit was causing trouble, and why. While in trance, the *noiade* would fall unconscious, and it was

A Saami man sings out in the middle of a snowfield. The Saami have their own special, light-hearted form of song, known as a joik, which is sung unaccompanied. This makes it ideal for the traveling herders, who could not carry heavy instruments around with them. ▶

said that his soul was traveling in another world among the spirits who live there, in order to fight with them. He could save the life of a sick person by rescuing the person's stolen soul, or find the whereabouts of lost reindeer or of a dangerous bear.

Christians from the south were already making occasional contact with the Saami in the Middle Ages and by the seventeenth and eighteenth centuries many Saami had become Christians. But many others resisted and remained faithful to their beliefs in the spirit world of *noiade*. The Scandinavian missionaries burned the *noiade*'s

The old Saami *noiade* used a flat drum covered with figures of people, animals, the sun, and the stars. The drum was used for trances, and also to divine, or guess the future. The *noiade* would place a small piece of horn on the skin and beat the drum. As the piece of horn moved around the figures, the *noiade* would explain what this movement meant. For instance, if the horn stopped by the picture of a bear, it might mean that the person who had asked for the divination would meet a bear. Other places where the horn stopped would indicate whether this encounter would be successful or dangerous.

◀ *A wooden church in Finland. During the seventeenth and eighteenth centuries there was great conflict between Christian missionaries, their converts, and those Saami who continued to believe in the spirit world of their first religion. Today, many Saami are Christians, while among others interest in the traditional beliefs is growing.*

A mother and daughter selling traditional handicrafts to tourists in Sweden. Lapland is often advertised as "Europe's Last Wilderness," and tourists come from abroad as well as from the towns of Scandinavia. Tourism contributes a lot of money to the local economy, but tourists can also be a nuisance (see page 17). ▶

drums and sometimes killed the *noiade*. In Russia, too, the authorities encouraged missionaries to convert the Saami. The old religion was considered the work of the devil and even now many Christian Saami feel uncomfortable talking about it.

The strongest Christian influence came from a priest named Laestadius, at the beginning of the nineteenth century. His version of Christianity, called Laestadianism after him, is now widespread among Saami (except for the Saami in Russia and a few in Finland, who belong to the Russian Orthodox Church). Though there were some *noiade* left until the middle of the last century, and some ideas about spirits and herbal medicine may still survive to this day, the old religion has entirely disappeared.

Laestadianism is a form of Christianity that the Saami share with Swedish, Norwegian, and Finnish people of the region. This shows how difficult it can be to make a clear distinction between Saami and others. Some people say that the old Saami *noiade*'s trance lives on in the mood of excitement that can sweep through a Laestadian congregation at church meetings.

Today, a few people have begun trying to revive the Saamis' own original religion and there is growing interest in it as an important part of Saami history. "This is our very own, our original religion," people say, "We didn't get it from anybody else. In this way, our forefathers showed their respect for nature and for the world around them." In one village in Norway, a school crafts teacher makes copies of the old *noiade*'s drums for playing; another Saami who lives in Oslo, the Norwegian capital, has become known as a *noiade* and gives lectures at home and abroad; in northern Sweden there is a theater group formed jointly of Saami and Iroquois (North American Indian) members.

LANGUAGE AND EDUCATION

It is at school that the problems of Saami culture appear most sharply. Until recently, the course of study in each of the four countries has been largely decided by non-Saami in the south and has often not taught children what they need to know if they are to continue their cultural traditions. In particular, children who will go on to work in reindeer herding or fishing need to gain a very detailed understanding of animals and nature. This cannot be learned in the

Stallo monsters

In Saami mythology, the Stallos were a race of monsters who ate humans. Stallo women sucked the strength out of people through an iron pipe. Many stories tell of encounters in which Saami heroes trick the Stallos and destroy them:

Once, the Saami and a Stallo were playing blind man's bluff on the surface of a frozen lake. Every time the Stallo caught a person he bit his catch hard and said "That's good, I'll have some meat for tomorrow!" So the Saami lured him toward some holes they had cut in the ice and he fell in. The Stallo called to his wife to bring her iron pipe, kill the Saami, and rescue him before he froze to death. But the cunning Saami placed the mouthpiece of her pipe in the fire, so when she put it to her mouth to suck their lives out, she sucked in fire and died. So the Saami all survived.

◀ *Norwegian and Swedish Saami meet on the roadside. Some wear traditional costume, others do not: what links them, by allowing them to understand each other, is the Saami language. Very few Saami schoolchildren are taught in their own language, and some people are worried that it may slowly disappear.*

A Saami school in Norway. These reindeer herders' children are boarders, since their parents spend much time on the move with their animals. The children will join their parents for the holidays, but for the rest of the year they learn subjects that are far removed from the reindeer herder's life. ▶

classroom alone, but must also be learned from experience of doing this kind of work.

In many areas, children from outlying farms and tents have sometimes had to stay in boarding schools far from their families and their own way of life, which has made children and their parents very unhappy. This has been a particular problem in Russia as well as in Scandinavia, though the boarding school system throughout the region is now being abolished or improved.

Saami activists see the Saami language as the key to the survival of Saami culture, although their opponents point out that simply printing something in Saami does not make it part of Saami culture. Governments have sometimes encouraged or forced Saami to speak the main language of the country in which they live. At other times, usually under pressure from the Saami themselves, they have supported the development of the Saami language. Even today, though each country provides some teaching in the Saami language at primary-school level, Saami pupils can generally not be taught in their own language throughout their entire school career. One problem is that even if the authorities are willing, there is still a shortage of suitable textbooks and teaching aids in the Saami language. Recently, the Saami in Norway and Sweden have benefited from programs designed to teach the children of immigrants from southern Europe and Asia in their own languages.

Why is it thought to be so important to be taught in one's own language? The people who want to preserve the Saami language argue that it allows a person to talk about things in a special way. They point out that in reindeer herding there are special Saami words for deer of different ages, color, and shapes, which cannot be translated into any other language. There are exact words in Saami to show how tame a deer is or how good it is at pulling sleds. In the same way, where English has only a few words to describe snow, Saami has many words for different kinds of snow. These words say whether the snow is wet, hard, or even soft underneath a hard crust.

The Saami language can also serve as a symbol for people in the town who are unable to herd reindeer but who still want to feel Saami. For someone who lives in a town it is impossible to live as a herder, but possible to learn how to speak Saami. Supporters of Saami argue that

◀ *Brother D'Andres Alariesto in his studio. Brother Alariesto is a famous painter who lives in the wilderness near Sodankyla, in Finnish Lapland. His table is made of tree trunks, and Russian religious icons hang on the walls behind him.*

using your own language allows you to share more fully in the thoughts of people who lived before you. This includes your own ancestors, as well as poets and other writers. Many Saami authors have written about their life and their landscape. The poet Valkeapaa has been translated into English and has an international reputation. But he has nevertheless said, "I have never written with a view to translation, and some of what I write is intended primarily to be read only by Saami." His poems are almost impossible to translate because he uses the very clever word play found in songs called *joik* (pronounced yoik) which make sense only in Saami.

In some areas of life, Saami people have become so used to making do in the dominant language that they can be shocked when they hear their own language used. "We're not used to talking in Saami to doctors. We feel almost strange in our own language. When you're ill it's not so frightening to hear the same medical words in Norwegian. I remember we used to have a Saami doctor here who used plain Saami language. The patients were offended and got angry with him. He's left now."

5 Ethnic identity today

Saami culture today is under great pressure from the Norwegian, Swedish, Finnish, and Russian cultures and languages, as well as from the worldwide culture of rock music, videos, and Coca-Cola. Yet at the same time, many people in all four countries are more proud of being Saami now than at any time this century.

Though not many Saami are actually engaged in reindeer herding, this activity stands out as a symbol of Saami identity and is linked to a concern about rights to their own land and to the use of their own language in school and at home. Some of the Saami population are eager to protect their culture, while others want to give up their Saami identity and are hostile to any attempt to strengthen a separate Saami culture. These conflicting attitudes are reflected more and more in politics.

Several times in recent years the Saami have been forced to think hard about their ethnic identity. Three examples are: differences of opinion about the Alta hydroelectric dam, the Chernobyl nuclear disaster, and the campaigns for the Saami to have control of their own land.

▲ *A view of Kiruna, the main industrial town in Swedish Lapland. The town is built on a huge deposit of iron ore, which is exported to the rest of the world along the railroad to the port of Narvik on the Norwegian coast.*

◀ *An old reindeer herder in traditional dress. The Saami herders' life-style is threatened by the construction of hydroelectric dams on their traditional pastures: the dam across the Alta River, for example, made large areas of pasture inaccessible to the Saami (see maps on page 38).*

THE ALTA DAM

The first is the controversy over the Alta hydroelectric dam in northern Norway. There are numerous rivers in the mountains behind the town of Alta that could be harnessed to generate electricity, mostly for the big towns in the south. In the 1970s, the Norwegian government proposed to dam a river and flood an important area of reindeer pasture used by the local Saami herders. About a similar dam already completed elsewhere, an expert wrote: "The road runs through the spring pastures. It is there that the cows find the plants they must have so that they can give their calves milk. But the cows are easily frightened at calving time and because of the traffic the animals take off into the hills where it is colder and the pastures are poorer. The calves freeze to death up there even as they are born." The protests of the Saami were supported by Norwegian conservationists and others, and the case received a lot of publicity.

While the conservationists protested at the site of the dam itself, a group of Saami protesters traveled to Oslo, the capital of Norway, and pitched a traditional *lavvo* on the lawn of the Norwegian parliament. There, they began a hunger strike. This protest shocked public opinion in Norway, where most people had believed that the Saami minority were treated in a humane and decent way. The protesting Saami were claiming something that they believed the Norwegian government was not allowing them: the right to say how their own land should be used. The battle was not just over this one particular piece of pasture, where the livelihood of only a few reindeer herders was threatened. The choice between reindeer herding and hydroelectric power in any location, they said, must be made by the Saami themselves and not by the Norwegian government hundreds of miles away.

The Alta dam case became more than a consevation issue – it became an issue of Saami rights within the Norwegian state. Indigenous peoples in other countries far away, for example the Inuit and Cree in Canada, were involved in similar disputes with their own governments and they and the Saami protesters supported each other. In the end, the campaigners lost their case in court, but they succeeded in concentrating the world's attention on the issue in a way that would not be forgotten.

The Alta dam case had other long-term consequences. It was not simply a dispute between Norwegian and Saami. There were also differences between various groups of Saami. The protesters had claimed that the government's attack on reindeer herding was an attack on

▲ *At a demonstration against the proposed building of the dam across the Alta river, the slogan reads "The River Shall Live!" The tops of two lavvos are just visible over the top of the bank behind.*

Saami culture in general, which implied that herders represented all Saami people. But what about the 90 percent of Norwegian Saami who do not herd reindeer? Since they began doing more factory work and deep-sea fishing in power boats, the coastal Saami have had less and less in common with the inland herders. They not only dress and work like Norwegians, but they have also increasingly given up speaking the Saami language in favor of Norwegian. Only a few had host-guest relations with mountain Saami, while the majority felt they had less and less to do with the herders who drove reindeer across their territory each year, causing a great deal of upheaval and damage on the way. But the Alta dam campaigners, just like the tourist industry, still gave the impression that to be properly Saami you must be a reindeer herder. The coastal Saami, and even various other kinds of inland Saami, felt left out.

The Alta dam case brought a number of different opinions out into the open, supported by opposing political parties. Some Saami felt that it showed how necessary it was for the Saami people to have special legal protection as an aboriginal minority people. Those who believed most strongly in the central importance of reindeer herding for Saami culture opposed the dam especially strongly.

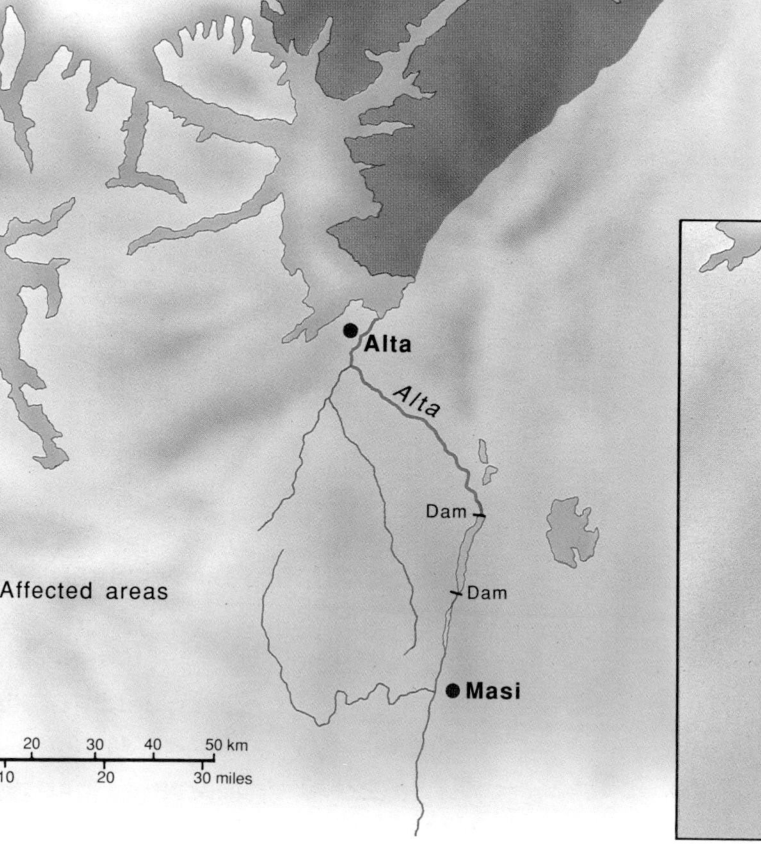

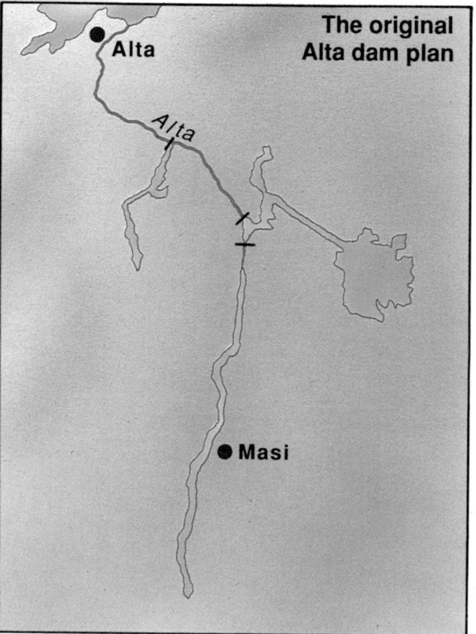

◀ *The map shows pastures, traditionally used by Saami reindeer herders, that could no longer be reached when the Alta dam was built. The migration routes were blocked.*

▲ *The Alta dam protests caused divisions among the Saami. This man is a Saami, although he is not dressed in traditional clothing and does not herd reindeer. Many people became angry that the Alta case focused attention on the reindeer herders and their rights, even though other Saami would benefit from the electricity the dam would provide.*

Other Saami said that their people should not receive any special privileges but should "remain citizens of the mother country Norway on an equal basis." In particular, they felt that the Saami should share land and water with the other, numerous non-Saami inhabitants of the region. This means that they supported the building of the Alta dam and argued that this kind of development was equally good for the Saami themselves, who also benefit from electricity and other comforts in their homes.

THE CHERNOBYL DISASTER

Another event that greatly affected the Saami and their ideas about themselves was the nuclear disaster at Chernobyl, in Ukraine. In April 1986, a reactor in a nuclear power plant caught fire and the wind scattered dangerous radioactive substances across Ukraine, Poland, and Scandinavia. Some of them also reached other countries. These radioactive substances cause cancer, and crops, vegetables, animals, and people were contaminated all through this area.

The damage was worst where rain brought the radioactive substances down to earth. In Britain, meat from sheep in certain montainous areas was declared unsafe for people to eat for several years. The rain also fell particularly heavily on central Scandinavia, including the western parts of Saami territory. The effect on the Saami reindeer herders in the area was devastating. Not only did these people depend on selling reindeer meat to the shops for their living, they also ate much of it themselves. They were particularly exposed to radiation because in winter the reindeer feed mainly on lichen, and lichen absorbs a large amount of radioactive substances from the air. Since it takes thirty years for lichen to regrow completely, this

▲ *The meltdown at the nuclear power plant in the Ukraine (top) in 1986 made the nearby region too dangerous to live in and scattered radioactive contamination over hundreds of miles. The effect of this contamination was disastrous for the Saami: the bottom picture shows reindeer meat being tested for radioactivity.*

Preparing a reindeer carcass in Sweden. Saami prefer to slaughter deer in the autumn and winter, when the meat tastes best after the deer feed on the summer pasture. The Chernobyl accident scared away customers for reindeer meat, and the Saami did not get enough compensation from the government, so many of them suffered financially. The reindeer herders continued to eat the meat, despite the threat to their health, partly because they couldn't afford to do anything else. ▶

contamination will last for a long time. The radioactivity is concentrated in the flesh of the reindeer and then enters the bodies of humans who eat the meat. Even Saami who did not depend on reindeer were affected as fish, berries, and even drinking water were poisoned.

When the time came for the slaughter in the autumn of 1986, many of the reindeer carcasses were found to be above the safety limit set by the Norwegian government. A large number of deer had to be destroyed because they were too contaminated, and compensation was paid by the government to the herders. None of the governments of the region was prepared for this kind of disaster and the people received such conflicting advice from different experts that they did not know what to believe. In Norway, for example, many people lost confidence in the government when the safety limit was raised from 600 becquerels (a unit of radioactivity) per kilogram (2.2 pounds) of meat to 6,000 becquerels. Since very many deer gave a higher reading than 600 becquerels, the original limit would have required the slaughter of an enormous number of reindeer, at a huge cost to the government in compensation. But the new limit of 6,000 greatly reduced the number of deer that had to be killed and so also reduced the government's bill. As Saami themselves put it at the time, "Whom can we believe? How can 600 becquerels be dangerous yesterday and safe today? Is it safe to eat meat at 5,999 becquerels?"

The Chernobyl accident has had serious consequences for the traditional position of reindeer herding at the heart of Saami culture. How could people raise reindeer and eat the meat if they believed it would make them sick or kill them? These Saami were forced to choose between protecting their bodies by giving up reindeer and losing their culture, and defending their culture by continuing to eat reindeer, but putting their health at risk. In addition, the technical complexities of monitoring and decontamination procedures meant that the reindeer herders' own knowledge of nature and animals was not enough to cope with the situation in which they found themselves. At every turn, they were forced to rely on the scientific knowledge of outside experts. It will take a long time to learn the full consequences of the Chernobyl accident, either for health or for culture. But around that time there was a noticeable increase in Saami cultural activity, as though the disaster had brought some people to the realization that their culture was valuable to them after all, but fragile and easily damaged.

INCREASING POLITICAL ACTIVITY

There have been increasing demands from some Saami for greater control over their own affairs. The Saami of Finland have had a parliament of their own since 1976 but in the other countries where Saami live this has not happened. It was largely as a result of the Alta dam case that a Saami Rights Commission was set up in Norway

◀ *Saami on their way to attend a meeting in Swedish Lapland. Many Saami make a point of wearing traditional clothes at public meetings, especially if the meeting is to discuss their demands and rights.*

A distinctive wooden church in Finnish Lapland. Some groups of Saami in Finland belong to the Russian Orthodox religion: this church is in a typical Russian style and the couple in the picture are proudly displaying a Russian icon, one of the chuch's treasures. ▶

in 1980, bringing together representatives from numerous organizations, including ones with totally opposed views. In 1982, Sweden also set up a Saami Rights Commission. In both countries, the commissions recommended setting up a Saami parliament. The Saami parliament in Norway was opened in Kautokeino by the King of Norway, while the parliament in Sweden is due to be set up soon.

The Saami in Russia do not yet have a parliament of their own, though they are members of Russia's Association of Northern Peoples. This was set up in Moscow in April 1990 and brings together about 30 indigenous peoples from across the whole of northern Russia. The Saami are the westernmost of these peoples, who include the Siberian Inuit on the Bering Strait, facing Alaska. Some of these peoples speak languages distantly related to Saami.

No one is sure how to count how many Saami there are, and the boundary between Saami and

▲ *A Saami and his dog out fishing in a Norwegian fjord*

non-Saami is not always clear. In particular, most coastal Saami as well as many others have forgotten the Saami language or do not use it in their everyday lives. This is true even of some reindeer herders. So who is to to be considered Saami and allowed to vote in elections for the Saami parliament? Clearly, those who still speak Saami should be able to vote. But very many who do not speak the language still consider themselves to be Saami and may even wish they could learn the language if only there were an opportunity. There is no easy answer to the question of who is or is not Saami, but the electoral roll aims to include everyone whose parents or grandparents spoke Saami.

If the right to vote for a Saami parliament is seen as something worth having, the number of people who identify themselves as Saami will increase. But in both Norway and Sweden, Saami and their supporters have been disappointed because these parliaments do not have the power to veto new projects such as the Alta dam. The new Saami parliaments are allowed to give their opinion and to advise the Norwegian and Swedish governments, but these governments do not have to take any serious notice of Saami opinion. So the main complaint of the Saami, that they are not able to control what is done to their land, remains unchanged. As one speaker put it, "We have never given away our right to the areas which our forebears inhabited for thousands of years. We have never sold our open spaces or our water. No one has conquered our rivers and shores in war. But nevertheless, people from outside have come and taken our land. In the Middle Ages, the

King's bailiffs took all the game from our woods as tax. Later, industries were built up on ore from Saami land. Nobody asked us. And on those occasions when they have asked, they haven't listened to our advice. Many of our people have given up."

At the moment, what it means to be Saami remains unclear and full of conflict. To take Norway alone, the parliament has done little to sort out the disagreements between those Saami who want to live under the Norwegian government on the same terms as all other Norwegian citizens, and those who insist that as an indigenous people the Saami must have special rights in the regions where they live. It is becoming more and more necessary to know the main language of one's own country since few non-Saami can speak Saami.

At the same time, the demands of many Saami for greater local control over their lands echo calls heard throughout the world. The Saami, like many other peoples, want to keep their land from being ruined by pollution or industrial development. We can only wait and see if the Saami parliaments will succeed in making the voice of the Saami heard, and whether they succeed in making the breakthrough from just giving advice to making laws.

On the move in Norway. Only children who travel with their parents, and experience both the hardships and the freedom of the open land, are likely to continue the tradition of reindeer herding. ▶

Glossary

Aboriginal people The people who inhabited a country first, before other peoples arrived.
Anthropologist A researcher who studies the different ways of life and ideas of the peoples of the world.
Archaeologist A reasearcher who studies the ways of life of the peoples of the past, through the things they have left behind such as old tools and bones. For example, archaeologists dig through the sites of old camps to find out what the people who lived there did many years ago.
Arctic The Arctic is strictly only the region north of the Arctic Circle, which lies at 66°33' North. Anthropologists usually define it as bigger than this area, and include among the Arctic peoples many who live outside the Arctic Circle.
Becquerel A unit used to measure radioactivity.
Basques A people who live in the mountains of northern Spain and southwestern France. The Basques have their own language called Euskardi, and many of them feel that they should have their own country instead of being part of France and Spain.
Bretons A people who live in northwestern France and have their own language which is close to Welsh. Some Bretons want their land to be distinct from the rest of France.
Castrate Remove all or some male sexual organs in order to make an animal more tame.
Corral An enclosed area used to contain a herd of animals.
Culture The whole set of ideas and ways of behaving that make one people different from another.
Davveli A direction: away from the reindeer's winter pasture, toward the coast.
Decoy Something to attract an animal without frightening it.
Ethnic To do with a particular people; ethnic identity means a people's sense of having a culture of their own that makes them different from other peoples.
Fjord A deep inlet on the Norwegian coast, often with very steep sides.
Forebear An ancestor; an older relative.
Gorbachev Leader of the Soviet Union (U.S.S.R.) from 1985 to 1990, who began the reforms that led to the downfall of Communism.
Immigrant A person who comes to live in one country or area after having lived in another.
Inuit A people spread along the Arctic coasts of Greenland, Canada, Alaska, and Siberia; sometimes still called Eskimo by outsiders, though they themselves do not like this name.
Joik A kind of improvised Saami song.
Lasso A length of rope with a loop at the end. The loop is thrown over the antlers of an animal to capture it.
Lavvo A tepee used by reindeer herders on the move.
Lichen A plant without leaves, somewhat like moss; essential food for reindeer in winter when leaves are dead.
Minority A distinct group of people who are outnumbered by others around them.
Noiade A Saami shaman.
Nomad A person who does not live permanently in one place but who moves with the herds from place to place with the seasons.
Scandinavia The countries Norway, Sweden, Denmark, and Iceland, whose majority peoples all speak similar languages; sometimes Finland is also included.
Shaman A spirit medium who communicates with spirits by going into a trance.
Si'ida The traditional Saami work unit, composed of several families and their herds;

among coastal Saami, the men who work together on a fishing boat.

Trance A state of mind similar to hypnosis in which a person may be unaware of their surroundings but is able to see or understand things she or he would not normally see.

Tundra Landscape in the Arctic with low-growing shrubs and grasses but no trees.

Welsh A people from west-central Britain (Wales) who have their own language. Historically, many Welsh have wanted to restore the independence of Wales. They call themselves Cymraeg and their country Cymru.

Further information

Arctic Institute of North America
University of Calgary
2500 University Drive N.W.
Calgary, AB T2N 1N4
Canada

International Work Group for Indigenous Affairs
Fiolstraede 10, DK-1171
Copenhagen
Denmark

Nordiskt Samiskt Institut (Norwegian Saami Institute)
Box 220, N-9520 Guovdageaidnu, Kautokeino
Norway

Sameparlamentet (Saami Parliament)
SF-99870 Inari
Finland

Riksorganisationen Same Atnam
Box 4, S-933 00 Arvidsjaur
Sweden

Further reading

An enormous number of books have been written about the Saami. Your local public library or school library may have books not mentioned here. Books about Norway, Sweden, or Finland sometimes contain chapters about the Saami. Remember that in older books, the Saami are called Lapps. The International Work Group for Indigenous Affairs in Copenhagen, Denmark, also publishes a series of reports and newsletters in English. These often contain news items about the struggles of Saami, Inuit, and other peoples to protect their own land and culture.

Aldis, Rodney. *Polar Lands*. Ecology Watch. New York: Dillon Press, 1992.
Bullen, Susan. *The Arctic and Its People*. People and Places. New York: Thomson Learning, 1994.
Garrett, Dan. *Scandinavia*. World in View. Austin: Raintree Steck-Vaughn, 1991.
James, Barbara. *Conserving the Polar Regions*. Conserving Our World. Austin: Raintree Steck-Vaughn, 1990.
Lambert, David. *Polar Regions*. Morristown, NJ: Silver Burdett Press, 1987.
Reynolds, J. *Far North: Vanishing Cultures*. San Diego: Harcourt Brace Jovanovich, 1992.

Index Numbers in **bold** refer to pictures as well as text.

Alfred the Great 6, 7
Alta hydroelectric project 36-39, 44
Arctic Circle 9, 11
Association of Northern Peoples 43

calving 23
Chernobyl 39-42
  compensation for Saami 41
  contamination of reindeer meat 41
clothing **4**, **19**, **26**, 27, **31**
cloudberries 11
communications 12, 15

diet 10

education 32-**33**

farming 16
fjords 15
fishing **7**, **16**, 38
  cost of running a fishing boat 16
frostbite, traditional cure 17

Gorbachev 8

handicrafts **28**
hydroelectric projects *see Alta*

joiks 34

Kiruna, Sweden **35**

language 32-34
lassos 4, 46
lavvos **5**, **19**, 23, 37
lichen 9, 10, 40-41
  radioactive contamination of 41

marfi (blood sausage) 20
midnight sun 9
migration of reindeer herds 13, **17**, 21-**24**
myths
  origin of stars 27
  Stallo monsters 32

night clubs 19, 34
Nordic Saami Council 8
Nordic Saami Institute 8

Ottar, Norwegian chief 6, 7

reindeer
  chocolate-loving **19**
  origin of 13
  slaughter **10**, **41**
religion 28-32
  Laestadianism 31
  missionaries 31
  revival of traditional religion 31-32
  traditional 28-31

Saami
  coastal 5, 14-17, 18
  forest 12
  lake 5, 14
  mountain 5, 13
  number of Saami 6, 8
  origins of the Saami 6

Saami parliaments
  Finland 42
  Norway 43
  Sweden **42**, 43
  voting qualification 44
seasons 10-11
si'ida 20, 22, 25
skis 12
snowmobiles 4, 12, 18
Stallo monsters 24, 32

Tacitus (Roman historian) 7
tourism 16, 17
tree line 9
tundra 9

urban areas 18

Valkeapaa (Saami poet) 34

World War II 19